Maybe That's Autism

by Taylor Crowe and Leah Ulrich

TaylorCrowe.com
Art-ism, LLC

Credits:
Illustrations: Taylor Crowe
Text and Watercolor: Leah Ulrich
Creative Director: Leah Ulrich

ISBN: 978-0-615-83167-1

This book is dedicated to the memory of my father, David Crowe, whose love and devotion gave my life hope, opportunity, and purpose in a world once thought not possible. He always believed in me, never gave up on me, and helped make my life what it is today. *Thanks, Dad.*

— *Taylor Crowe*

Hi, I'm Conrad. I was excited for our first day of school. That was the first time I saw Alex.

"Alex! Stop! Look both ways!" screeched a woman in a red car.

People slammed on their brakes, as a boy ran in front of them.

Alex walked into the classroom.

Mrs. Remley said, "Hello, Alex. Are you ready for your first..." Before she finished, he turned and ran out the door.

"What's wrong with him?" asked Dmitri, one of my friends.

"I don't know," I shrugged. "Maybe he's shy?"

"Yeah but...Do you remember hearing about a new boy with autism? Maybe that's him."

I wanted to meet him. I was curious.

"Hi, I'm Conrad. What's your name?"

There was no response. Alex wouldn't look at me.
Blair came up to meet him, too.

He finally answered, "Alex." Then he got up and
walked away.

I didn't know what to think. Had we done
something wrong?

Alex walked to the
bulletin board to look
at a picture of a tree
loaded with paper apples.

The bell rang and we went
to our seats. Mrs. Remley
walked Alex from the
bulletin board to his seat,
next to mine.

"Everyone," Mrs. Remley said, "I would like you to meet your new classmate, Alex. Alex has autism. He's just the same as everyone else in this room, except that some things are difficult for him to do."

"GOOD MORNING!" boomed a voice
over the intercom.

Alex covered his ears tightly with his hands
as if something was hurting him.

"I can't stand loud noises!" Alex whined.
"They make my ears feel bad."

No way! I didn't think he was joking,
but I wasn't sure. Maybe this was his autism.

"Good morning, class," our teacher said.

"Good morning, class," repeated Alex.

"I'm Mrs. Remley."

"I'm Mrs. Remley," Alex repeated.

It seemed that Alex was a funny guy…except he looked confused.

"Stop repeating," I warned.

"I'm Mrs. Remley…" He said again.

Okay, I thought, maybe he couldn't help it.

Soon, our teacher passed out a math worksheet. I started doing the problems.

"Ugh! Why can't I get this?!" moaned Alex. He looked unhappy.

"Be quiet," said Dmitri as everyone turned to look at Alex.

"Alex, it's all right," Mrs. Remley gently explained. "You're doing fine. Just do the best you can, okay?"

"Okay," Alex said, but he still seemed unhappy.

In reading class, everyone took turns reading a
silly story out loud. Soon everyone was laughing,
but not Alex. Alex just sat there with a dazed look
and watched everybody else have a good time.

Things really changed in spelling class, though.

With every word she gave us, Alex just raised his hand and started spelling. At first, we got upset because we weren't getting a turn, but then it was funny. Mrs. Remley called out really hard words and Alex could spell all of them! He didn't understand the rules about waiting to be called on, but he sure could spell!

Maybe that's autism?

"It's time for science class!" said Mrs. Remley smiling. "Today we will talk about clouds and weather."

"Alex, do you like rain or sunshine?"

Alex didn't answer. Spelling was easy for him, but when she asked him a simple question it was like he couldn't think of the words to say.

Maybe that's autism?

The bell rang. Recess was early. It was supposed to be at 10:30, but the clock showed 10:20. What a fun surprise! As we hurried to the door, I noticed Alex still sitting at his desk.

8 - 8:45   MATH
8:45-9:30   READING
9:30-10:00   SPELLING
10-10:30   SCIENCE
10:30-10:45 RECESS
10:50-11:15 ART
11:20-12:00   LUNCH
12:05-12:50 GEOGRAPHY
12:55-1:30   HANDWRITING
1:30-2:15   P.E.
2:15-3:00   MUSIC

"Come on, Alex! Let's go!" I said.

Alex didn't move. Worse yet, he started to cry. What could be wrong now? It was recess!

Something wasn't right. It had something to do with time because he kept looking at the clock.

Maybe that's autism?

Mrs. Remley brought Alex
out to the playground. He
stood and watched, then
ran toward the swings.

Maybe he was shy
around new people, and
this way he could play
by himself.

After playing tag, I asked
my friend Yao to come
with me to the swings.

"Sure!" he said.

He probably didn't know
what to think about Alex.
I didn't either, but we each
took a swing next to him.

It was so fun!

We had a great conversation with Alex for the rest of recess. Alex, Yao, and I were swinging, laughing, and talking about movies and video games. For the first time all day, Alex was really happy. Talking was easy for him! He seemed like a new friend.

Recess ended.
    By now we all had
questions about Alex.
What was this thing
called autism?

"No, no. It's not like a cold. You can't catch autism," Mrs. Remley told us. "Alex was born that way, and he can't help it."

Ok, good to know, I thought. I had been wondering the same thing myself.

I suddenly realized how confusing things were for Alex and us. We didn't understand Alex, and he didn't seem to understand us, either. It didn't seem fair.

Back in class, Alex
surprised everyone again.
"Oh, no! No, no, NO!"
he screamed. "No!!!"

"What's wrong?" Mrs. Remley asked as she rushed over to him.

Alex was very unhappy about something in the classroom. This time, he cried and screamed.

Watching Alex was kind of scary. Finally, Alex started to calm down, but something was still wrong.

"Alex, are you all right?"
I asked quietly.

   "No," he said, glancing
toward one wall in the
classroom.

   To my surprise, I
discovered that during
recess, Mrs. Remley
had changed the
bulletin board!

"Hey, is it the bulletin board?" I asked.

"Yes," Alex replied. "She took apples out of the tree."

I couldn't believe this would upset Alex that much, but then again, Alex was surprising us with all sorts of things. Maybe that's autism?

As we left the room for lunch, Alex was fine.

In the cafeteria, I thought about Alex. Alex seemed unpredictable. He ran away when he met new people. Loud noises hurt him. He liked to repeat what people said. He got upset easily when he couldn't do something. He didn't laugh at the funny story like the rest of the class. He didn't want to talk when it was his turn. But he was happy to blurt out answers when it wasn't. He was great at spelling words! He liked to talk and swing. Set times seemed important to him and changes were bad. It was like he wanted things exactly a certain way.

Maybe that's autism.

The best part of the day happened at the end of music class. Alex walked over to the piano and started playing. It was fantastic! Alex could play the piano better than anyone! Our teachers looked at each other, then back at Alex with huge smiles on their faces. Everyone was smiling. Alex was amazing!

The bell rang. I saw the woman from the red car talking to Mrs. Remley. She must be his mother. Alex was standing next to her, smiling and flapping his hands as if he was excited.

The first day of school was over. It was a super day... Maybe, I made a new friend!

And That's Autism

- The first page of the book shows Alex running in front of cars. Children with autism may have a lower sense of danger.

- On the next pages, we see Alex exhibiting two common traits of autism: avoidance of direct eye contact and shyness. A child on the spectrum might leave the room or go to another area in the room to avoid this sort of discomfort.

- A child with Autism Spectrum Disorder (ASD) may require assistance from a teacher or friend to move to a new activity. They can easily become distracted by conversation, background noise, etc.

- Stimming is a behavior a child may exhibit to help calm themselves such as chewing on a pencil or flapping their hands.

- Loud sounds can cause discomfort and overstimulation.

- Echolalia is the behavior of repeating words or phrases.

- Autistic children can become easily frustrated, loud, upset, or anxious.

- Humor, such as joking or sarcasm, can be difficult to understand. A student might feel left out of a situation because it doesn't make sense.

- Spelling can be a fun subject for children with ASD because it does not require putting words together in sentences. Whereas conversation can be difficult.

- Set schedules are important. Changes are sometimes stressful.

- Just like with Alex, swinging can be relaxing. It can even help someone with autism become talkative.

- In every classroom, the environment will periodically change, the reasons for the change may not be apparent. This can be very upsetting for an autistic child. For example, when Mrs. Remley moved some apples out of the tree.

- As with Alex, some students are gifted in areas such as music, math, memory, and art.

About the Authors

Taylor Crowe and Leah Ulrich

Taylor Crowe is a graduate of the California Institute of the Arts, where he studied Character Animation.

Leah Ulrich holds a BFA in Fine Arts from Southeast Missouri State University.

Taylor was diagnosed with autism as a preschooler. His artistic abilities were recognized in elementary school.

Leah's interests in art were also identified early. At age five, when asked to name her favorite toy, Leah replied, "My crayons."

This book was written by Leah with input from Taylor, drawing upon his childhood experiences. Taylor designed the characters and drew the illustrations. Leah used one of her favorite media, watercolors, to complete them.

This is their first book.

To learn more about
Taylor Crowe, visit —
taylorcrowe.com.
Feel free to ask questions
or leave comments.

www.ingramcontent.com/pod-product-compliance
Lightning Source LLC
Chambersburg PA
CBHW042107090426